# Trudy's Rock Story

**By: Trudy Spiller**

**Illustrations by: Jessika von Innerebner**

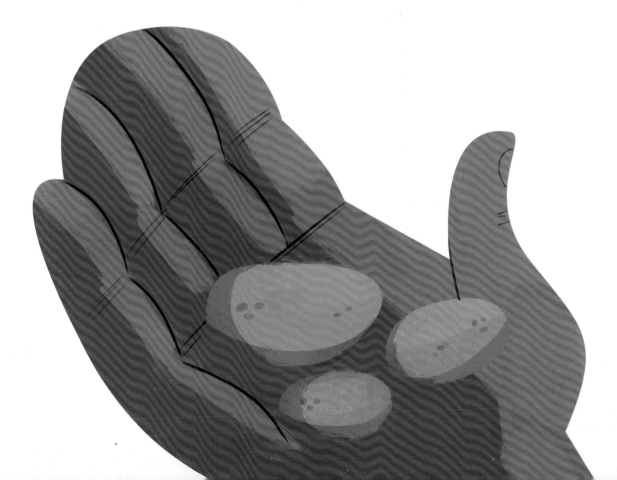

When Trudy was a little girl, she lived with her four sisters and three brothers.

Trudy's parents also shared their home with Trudy's *ts'iits* (grandmother).

They all lived together on a reserve not far from the Stegyoden mountains.

Each night, Trudy and her siblings would gather at their grandmother's feet and listen to her stories.

Trudy's *ts'iits* was a knowledge keeper. Through her stories, she passed on the wisdom of her ancestors. She made her friends and family knowledge keepers by asking them to remember and share the lessons she taught them.

We call this practice

*ant'imahlasxw.*

While the *ts'iits* told the children stories, she would mix soap berries together

until they stiffened like whipping cream. She called it *iss* (Indian ice cream) and it was delicious!

While *ts'iits* told the story, she scooped out *iss* and handed it to each child.

Trudy's *ts'iits* told a story about using the rocks of Mother Earth to solve a problem.

She told the children that when their hearts were heavy with sadness or anger,

they could use a rock to feel better.

Trudy listened very carefully.

"When you are out on a walk and you find a rock that catches your eye, it is meant for you," Trudy's *ts'iits* explained. "Hold that rock tightly in your hand and tell it what you are feeling, especially if you are upset."

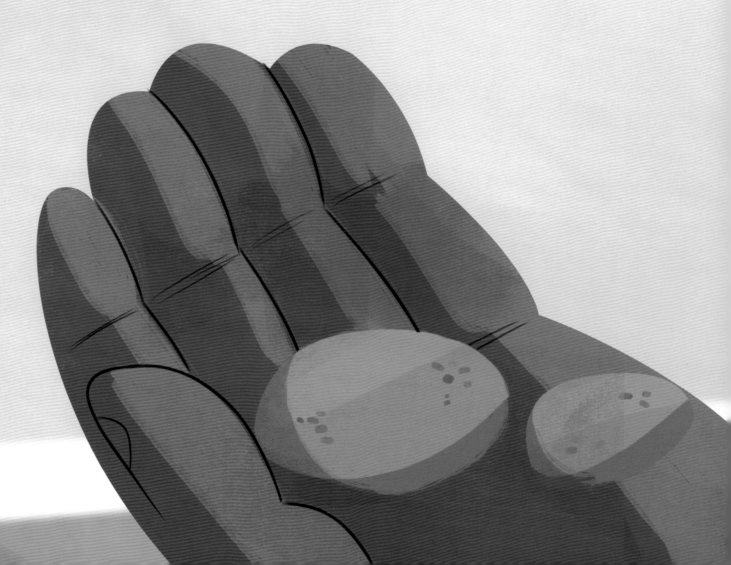

"When you feel less upset, you will know that you are ready to return it to Mother Earth. Then you can go put the rock back exactly where you found it."

One day, Trudy's grandmother heard yelling in the house. Trudy and her youngest brother were arguing loudly. He had teased her, and Trudy was really upset.

Instead of crying or sulking, Trudy told her grandmother that she was going for a walk. She put on her shoes and went into the woods.

She knew that she shouldn't go far and she

promised that she would be back by supper.

Trudy walked through the woods with tears running down her cheeks and her anger bubbling inside her.

She walked along the riverbank following its twists and turns.

She stopped at a bend in the river where there were lots of rocks.

Trudy thought about her grandmother's story,

about Mother Earth and about the rocks.

One of the rocks on the riverbank—a flat

rock about the size of her palm—caught her eye.

This rock seemed special. It called out to Trudy.

She felt as if the rock jumped out and

spoke to her like it wanted her to take it!

Trudy remembered what her grandmother had told her. This rock was one of Mother Earth's many gifts.

She could give her anger and sadness to the rock. So, Trudy clenched the rock tightly in

her fist and began talking to it as though it was someone she trusted and loved.

She talked so much that she didn't realize time had slipped away from her.

As the sun began to set, Trudy knew she had to get home soon.

She put the rock in her pocket for safekeeping.

Trudy noticed that she was already beginning to feel less angry.

She got back home just as the sun was disappearing behind the mountains. Her brothers and sisters were waiting for her to start dinner.

For the next few days, Trudy carried the
rock with her wherever she went.
Whenever she felt upset
she took out the rock in a
clenched fist and spoke to it.

She told it about the argument with her brother.

The more she spoke to it the better she felt.

Thanks to the rock and Mother Earth, Trudy's heart felt lighter.

She remembered what her grandmother had said

about returning the stone to its place in nature.

She told her grandmother she was going for another walk.

Trudy walked along the riverbank, following its

twists and turns—this time with a much lighter heart.

Soon, she came back to the bend in the river

where she had found her special rock.

Carefully, Trudy placed the rock back in the place
where she had found it. She returned it to Mother Earth,
who had given it to her when she needed it most.

She thanked the rock and she thanked Mother Earth

for helping her feel better when she was upset.

Trudy had learned a valuable lesson: Mother Earth would help her deal with

her negative feelings whenever she needed.

By giving back the rock, Trudy honoured Mother Earth's gift.

When Trudy returned home, she told her *ts'iits* about Mother Earth's gift and

how it had helped her release her anger and sadness. Her *ts'iits* hugged her tight

and told her that she was proud of her for understanding her story and its lesson.

"I know," *ts'iits* said, "that you truly are a knowledge keeper."

Today, Trudy sits with her own grandchildren and tells them her *ts'iits's* stories.

When she feels sad or angry, she finds a stone and tells it about what is bothering her.

She teaches her grandchildren to do the same, and she tells them to remember her stories

so that, one day, they can be knowledge keepers too.

Now you know Trudy's rock story—you are a knowledge keeper too.

If you feel sad or frustrated, you can find a stone

wherever you go.

When a rock speaks to you, hold it in your hand and share your feelings with it. You will soon feel better. When you feel better you should return the stone to Mother Earth.

Mother Nature has many wonderful gifts to share.

To find them, you must look, listen and honour the beauty that is all around you.

The end.

## Gitxsan Words & How to Say Them

Passing on stories from generation to generation = Ant'imahlasxw (ant-imah-a-sw)

Grandmother = ts'iits (t-ss-iitss)

Soapberries = iss (i-ss)

## Conversation Starters

What did Trudy's grandmother do?

Why did Trudy look for a stone?

What do you think Trudy said to the stone that she found?

Why did Trudy give the stone back to Mother Earth?

What do you do when you feel angry or sad?

Why is it good to let go of all the negative feelings?

Where would you go to find a special stone to hold?

Can you find your favourite stone in this book? What do you like about it?

Why do you think it is important to tell stories?

Now that you are a knowledge keeper, who do you want to tell this story to?

**About the Writer**

Trudy is part of the Gitxsan Nation in British Columbia
and belongs to the House of Gwininitxw of the Wolf Clan.
Trudy's traditional name, Lugaganowals, means a frog that is
always leaning or giving.

Trudy and her siblings were brought up to believe that children
are like flowers. Today, she helps families to grow and
flourish by sharing her knowledge of First Nation medicine,
food, dress, and practices. By sharing her stories,
Trudy makes knowledge keepers of us all.

A Medicine Wheel Education Book

We have more books for you!

Visit us at www.medicinewheel.education